Lila and Andy learn about

Climate Change

Understand Our Changing Planet

Kenneth Adams

Book Cover by Kenneth Adams
Illustrations and Images by Kenneth Adams
Illustrations and Images created with AI Assistance
First Edition 2025

ISBN: 978-1-998552-24-5

Your voice, your ideas,
and your dreams matter!

This book belongs to:

_____

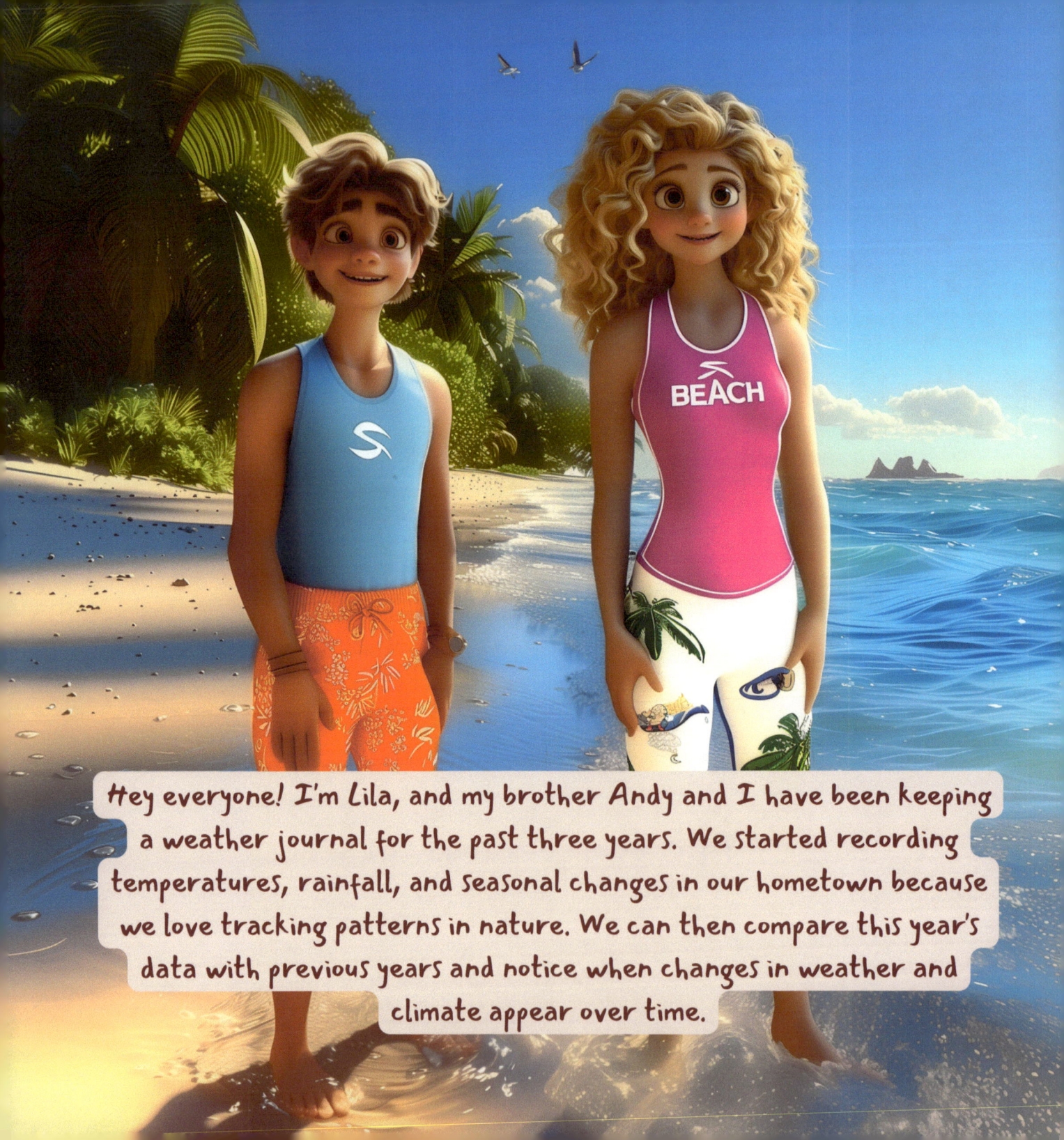

Hey everyone! I'm Lila, and my brother Andy and I have been keeping a weather journal for the past three years. We started recording temperatures, rainfall, and seasonal changes in our hometown because we love tracking patterns in nature. We can then compare this year's data with previous years and notice when changes in weather and climate appear over time.

On a recent visit to the Maldives, a chain of tropical islands in the Indian Ocean, known for their crystal-clear waters and coral reefs, we noticed that many of the coral reefs looked white and lifeless instead of the vibrant colors we expected to see. Our local guide explained that "coral bleaching" occurs when ocean temperatures remain too warm for too long.

We met fishermen who told us that the fish they used to catch in shallow waters now swim much deeper, and some islands we wanted to visit were partially underwater during high tide. Seeing all of this made us wonder about the bigger picture of how our planet's climate is changing, and how human actions might be contributing to these changes.

That's how we learned about climate change and its impact on ecosystems worldwide. Scientists study these changes by collecting data from oceans, ice cores, and weather stations to understand how human activities are warming our planet.

Today, we're thrilled to share what we've learned about climate change, its impact on various parts of the world, and the efforts people are making to address this global challenge.

Climate vs Weather

What makes "climate" different from "weather?"

The weather is what happens outside your window today. It may be sunny, or cloudy and rainy, or even cold and snowy. Climate, on the other hand, is the pattern of weather that occurs in a particular place over a long time. Think of it like this. "Weather" is one page in a storybook, while "Climate" is like reading the entire book from beginning to end to understand the whole story.

When you check if you need a jacket today, you're looking at the weather. When your family plans a beach vacation and knows it's usually sunny along the coast in June, they're thinking about the climate. Weather changes from day to day, but climate tells us what to expect over decades and centuries.

Our planet has different climate zones, each with its own unique weather patterns. The tropical zone near the equator stays warm all year. The polar zones near the North and South Poles stay mostly cold. The zones in between, where most people live, have seasons that change from warm to cold and back again.

Scientists study climate by collecting weather information over long periods, like thirty years or more. They measure temperatures, rainfall, wind patterns, and sunshine in thousands of places around the world. When they put all this information together, they can see how Earth's climate system works.

While there have been small changes to Earth's climate in the past, it has remained remarkably stable for thousands of years. This made it possible for forests to grow, rivers to flow where and how they do, and people to build cities and farms.

However, scientists have recently discovered that Earth's climate is changing much faster than it has in a very long time. Changes that used to take thousands of years are now happening in just decades.

Did you know that mountain glaciers in the Himalayas are melting twice as fast now as they were in the early 2000s, much faster than climate models predicted?

Did you know that scientists can tell what Earth's climate was like thousands of years ago by studying bubbles of ancient air trapped in ice from Antarctica and Greenland?

The Greenhouse Effect

For living creatures to stay alive, Earth's temperature must be just right, neither too warm nor too cold. The Earth stays warm enough for life because of something called the greenhouse effect. This process works like a lovely, woolly blanket keeping you warm at night, but instead of wool, Earth uses invisible gases in the atmosphere.

Here's how it works. Sunlight travels through space and reaches Earth's atmosphere. Most of this energy from the sun passes right through the air and warms the land and oceans. Then, Earth sends some of this heat back toward space. Certain gases in the atmosphere then trap some of the departing heat and radiate it back down to Earth, keeping our planet warm. The more gases there are to trap the heat, the warmer Earth becomes.

These special gases are called greenhouse gases because they work like the glass walls of a greenhouse. A greenhouse is a building made of glass that allows sunlight through. Gardeners use it to keep their plants warm so they don't die when the weather turns cold.

The Greenhouse Effect

Sun

1. Sunlight travels through space and reaches Earth, warming the land and oceans.
2. Some sunlight that hits Earth is reflected back into space, while some of it becomes heat.
3. Greenhouse gases trap some of this heat inside Earth's atmosphere, keeping Earth warm.

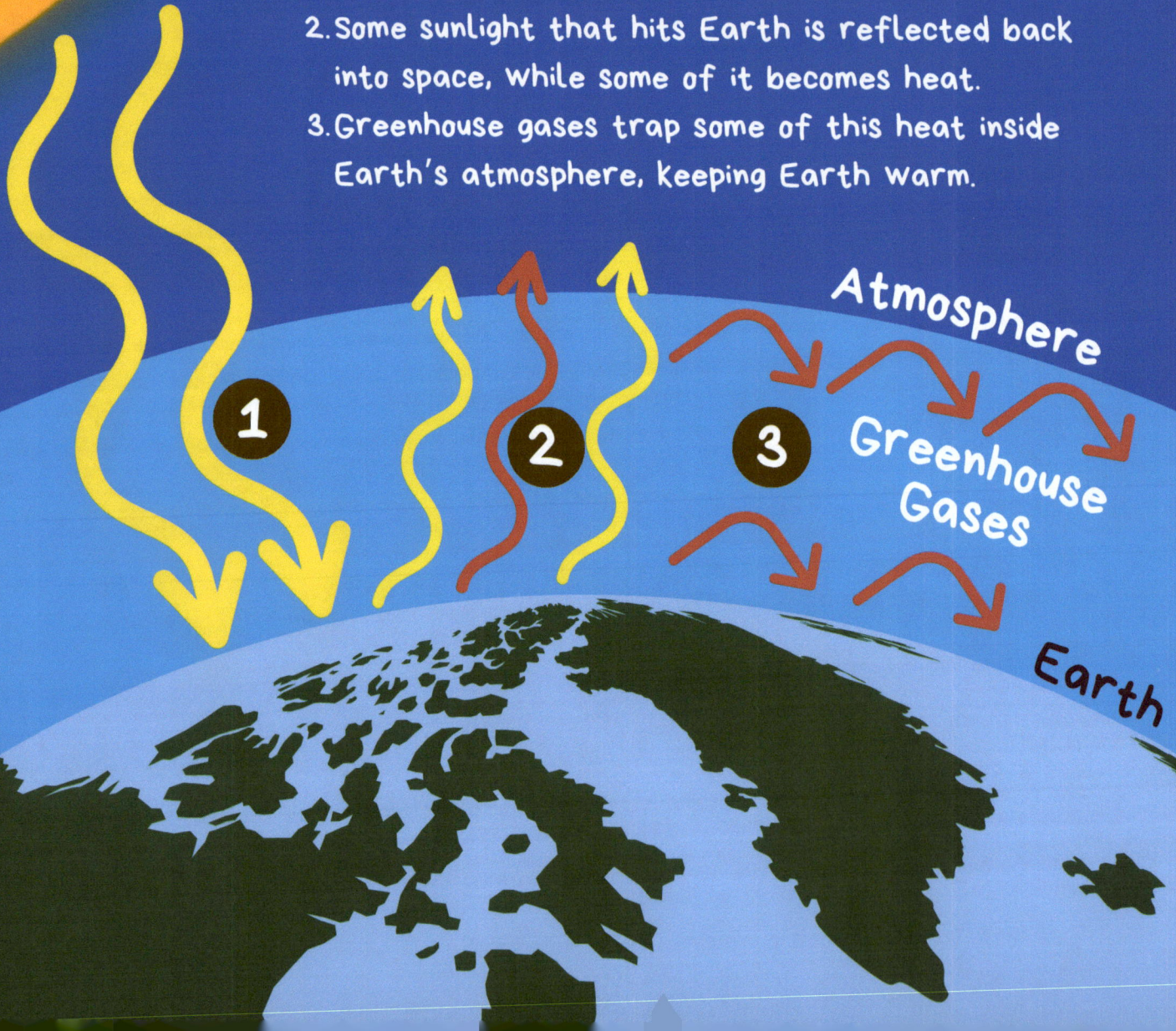

1

2

3

Atmosphere

Greenhouse Gases

Earth

The main greenhouse gases are water vapor, carbon dioxide, methane, and nitrous oxide. Without these gases, Earth would be about sixty degrees Fahrenheit (33 degrees Celsius) colder than it is now. Our planet would be frozen solid, like a giant ice ball floating in space.

Earth's distance from the sun, combined with the effect of greenhouse gases, is what makes Earth perfect for life. It's not too hot, like Venus, and not too cold, like Mars. For thousands of years, the greenhouse effect kept Earth's temperature steady, like a thermostat that maintains just the right temperature in your house.

But now, human activities are adding extra greenhouse gases to the atmosphere much faster than natural processes can remove them. As we said earlier, the more gases there are, the warmer the Earth becomes. It's like adding extra blankets to your bed. Eventually, you'll be much warmer than you want to be.

How Are We Adding Extra Greenhouse Gases To The Atmosphere?

The main reason greenhouse gases are increasing is that people burn fossil fuels for energy. Fossil fuels include things like coal, oil, and natural gas, which formed underground over millions of years. Every time someone drives a car, the engine burns gasoline and releases carbon dioxide. Every time a power plant burns coal to make electricity, it sends carbon dioxide into the atmosphere. When factories make steel, cement, or plastic, they often release greenhouse gases too.

Another source of greenhouse gases is agricultural activities. When farmers raise cattle and sheep, these animals produce methane gas.

And when people cut down forests to make room for cities or farms, there are fewer trees to absorb all the carbon dioxide from the air.

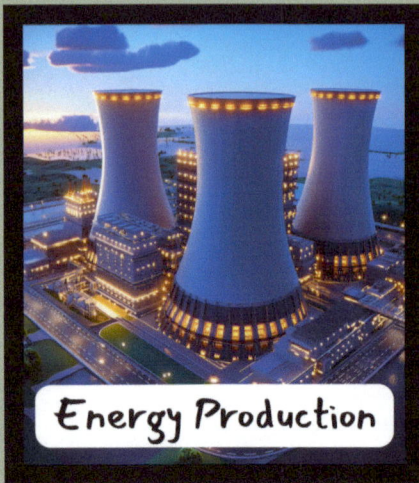
Energy Production

Manufacturing

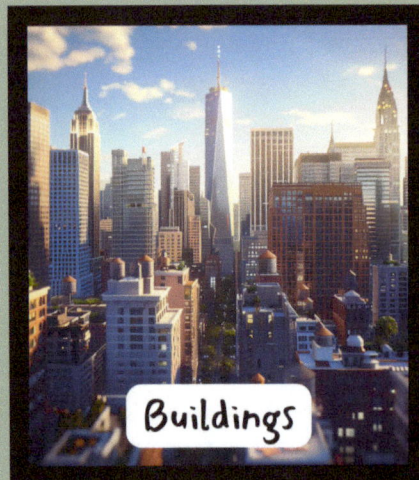
Buildings

Agriculture

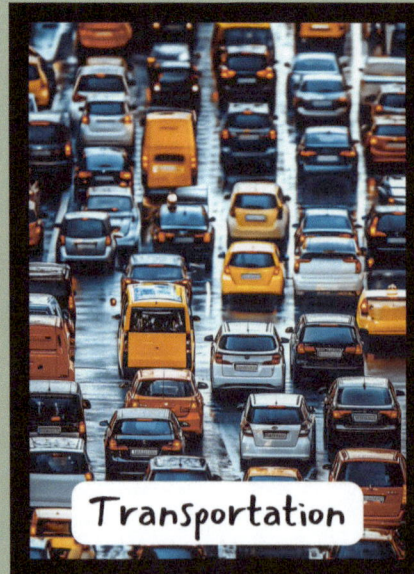
Transportation

It is clear to see that the main contributors to climate change are human activities that release greenhouse gases, particularly carbon dioxide, into the atmosphere.

Greenhouse gases are emitted by sectors as follows:

Electricity and heat generation from fossil fuels contributes 25% of global emissions.

Livestock farming, deforestation, and agricultural practices contribute 24% of global emissions.

Industrial processes, including cement, steel, and chemical production, contribute 21% of global emissions.

Road vehicles, shipping, and aviation contribute 24% of global emissions.

Heating, cooling, and cooking in residential and commercial buildings contribute 6% of global emissions.

Carbon dioxide from burning fossil fuels is the largest single contributor, making up about 76% of all greenhouse gas emissions.

The challenging thing is that carbon dioxide stays in the atmosphere for a very long time, even for hundreds of years. This means that even if people stopped adding carbon dioxide today, the extra greenhouse gases already in the atmosphere would continue to affect Earth's climate for many decades.

Scientists can measure exactly how much carbon dioxide is in the atmosphere using special instruments. They've discovered that there's now more carbon dioxide in the air than there has been for over 3 million years.

Climate Change We Can See

Climate change creates patterns that scientists can measure and that people around the world can see. While these changes happen little by little, they add up to big differences over time.

Climate change also affects different parts of the world in different ways, which is why some places experience more dramatic changes than others.

One of the clearest signs is that average temperatures around the world are getting warmer. The last decade included some of the warmest years ever recorded. This doesn't mean every single day is hotter, but when you look at temperature recordings over time, it shows more warm days and fewer extremely cold days.

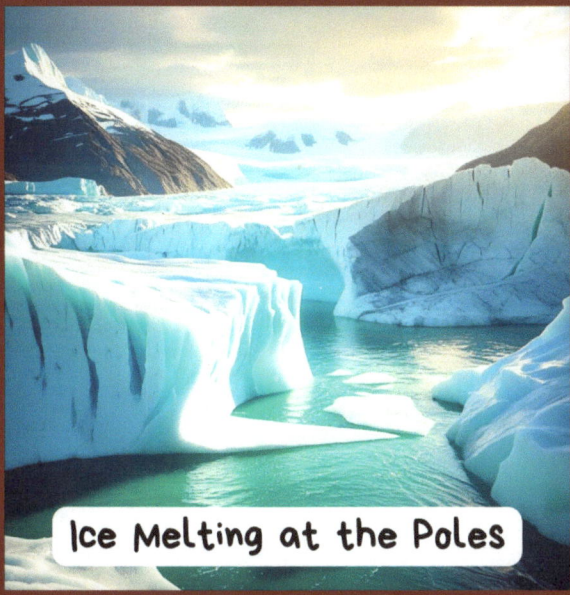

Ice Melting at the Poles

A Mountain Glacier

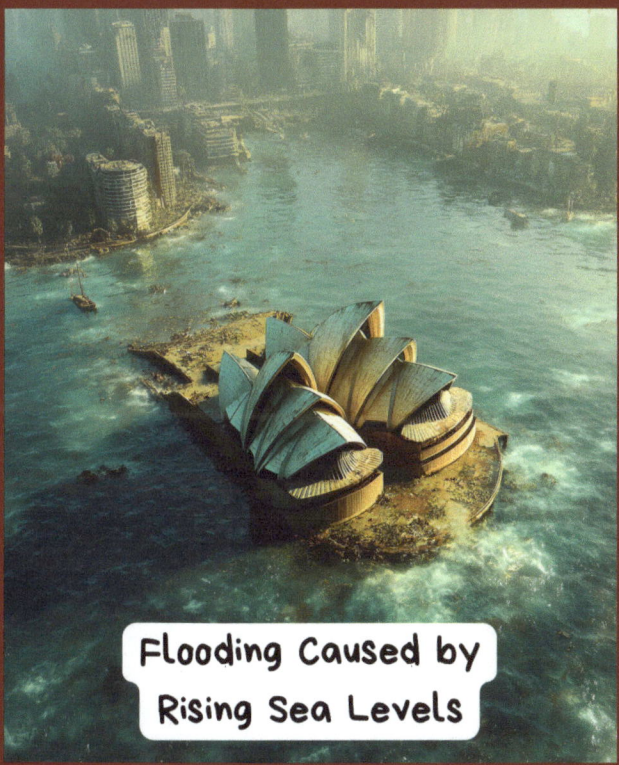

Flooding Caused by
Rising Sea Levels

Ice at the North and South Poles is melting faster than it forms. Mountain glaciers that took thousands of years to grow are shrinking and disappearing.

When this ice melts, it flows into the oceans, causing sea levels to rise slowly. Some coastal areas that were once dry now flood during storms.

You might notice these changes in your own neighborhood. Spring is arriving earlier in many parts of the world. Trees and flowers bloom sooner or at unexpected times, and leaves change color earlier or later than usual.

Birds migrate at different times than they used to, or you may see strange birds visiting your yard that never migrated to your city or town before.

Some families have noticed that their favorite hiking trails have snow that melts earlier each year, or that local ponds freeze later in winter than they used to.

Animals and plants that are adapted to specific temperature ranges are moving to different areas or changing their behaviors.

Ocean water is getting warmer, and when the ocean absorbs extra carbon dioxide from the atmosphere, it becomes more acidic, like adding lemon juice to water. This affects sea creatures that build shells and coral reefs that provide homes for many ocean animals.

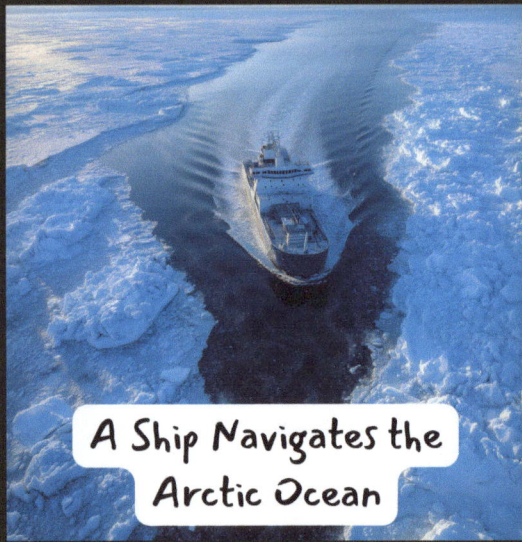
A Ship Navigates the Arctic Ocean

A Severe Thunderstorm

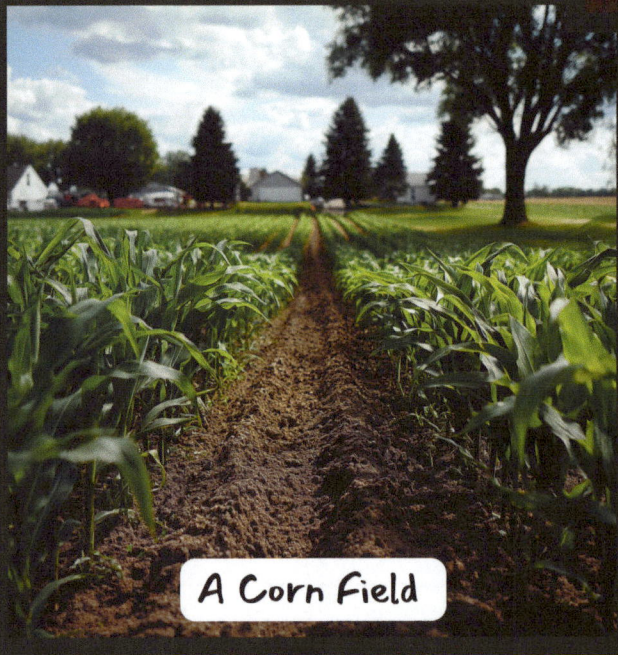
A Corn Field

People are observing changes, too. Farmers notice that crop-growing seasons are changing, ship captains see that Arctic sea ice forms later and melts earlier, and weather forecasters track more intense storm patterns worldwide.

A Tornado Touches Down

Weather patterns are changing, too. Some places that used to receive regular rainfall are now experiencing droughts. Other areas are getting more intense rainstorms, sometimes accompanied by hail as big as tennis balls. Hurricanes and tornadoes are also becoming more destructive as the atmosphere stores more energy from the extra heat.

Hail the Size of Golf Balls

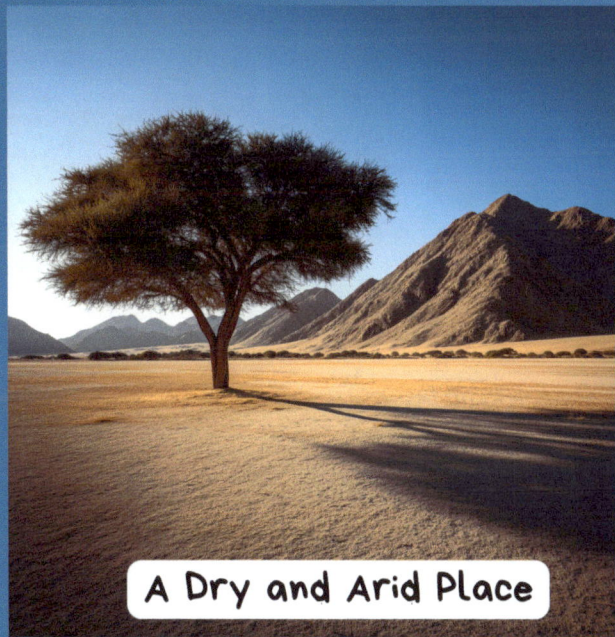
A Dry and Arid Place

How Can We Slow Down Climate Change?

Around the world, people are working on ways to reduce greenhouse gas emissions and adapt to the effects of climate change.

They invent new technologies, develop innovative methods to generate energy, and discover ways to remove carbon dioxide from the atmosphere.

Renewable energy sources are becoming more common and less expensive.

Solar panels capture energy from sunlight and turn it into electricity without producing any greenhouse gases.

Wind turbines use moving air to generate power.

Hydroelectric dams use flowing water to make electricity.

These renewable energy sources can provide all the power people need without burning fossil fuels.

A Wind Farm

Solar Panels in the Desert

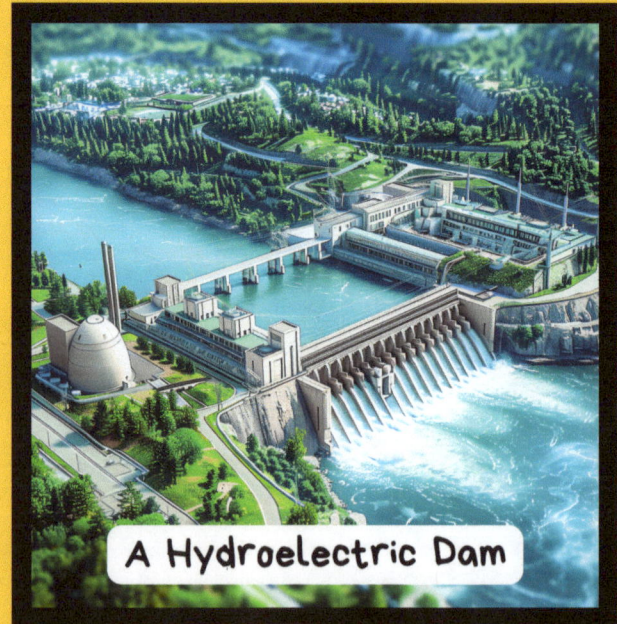

A Hydroelectric Dam

Electric cars, trucks, and buses are replacing vehicles that burn gasoline and diesel fuel.

These electric vehicles can travel hundreds of miles on a single charge and produce no emissions while driving.

As more renewable energy powers the electric grid, these vehicles become even cleaner.

Scientists are developing methods to capture carbon dioxide from the air by using big fans to blow air through a solution that catches the carbon dioxide from the air. They plan to convert it into useful products.

Some companies are improving natural processes, like planting forests and restoring wetlands that absorb carbon dioxide naturally.

Scientists are also working on coral restoration projects, growing new coral reefs in laboratories and transplanting them to damaged areas like the ones we saw in the Maldives.

Buildings are becoming more energy efficient through better insulation, smart heating and cooling systems, and LED lights that use less electricity. Some new buildings even produce more energy than they use by including solar panels and other renewable energy sources.

Farmers are adopting practices that store carbon in soil while growing healthy crops. They plant cover crops that absorb carbon dioxide, utilize precision agriculture to minimize fertilizer use, and develop new plant varieties that can thrive in the changing conditions.

Did you know that electric cars produce zero emissions while driving and can travel over 300 miles (480 km) on a single charge?

If all the cars in the world were electric, we could reduce global carbon emissions by about 16%!

Did you know that a single mature tree absorbs about 48 pounds (22 kg) of carbon dioxide every year?

Ethiopia once planted over 350 million trees in a single day to help fight climate change!

Cities around the world are creating climate action plans. They're adding bike lanes and public transportation, planting trees to provide shade and absorb carbon dioxide, and designing green spaces that can handle more intense rainstorms.

You and your family can also be part of the solution. Simple actions, such as walking or biking instead of driving short distances, turning off lights when leaving a room, recycling and reducing waste, and planting trees or gardens, all help reduce greenhouse gases. Some families choose to install solar panels on their homes, buy electric or hybrid cars, or support businesses that use clean energy.

Understanding climate change means understanding one of the most important challenges and opportunities of our time. The science clearly shows that our activities on Earth are adding greenhouse gases to the atmosphere faster than natural processes can remove them, and this is warming our planet and changing weather patterns.

Climate change is a challenge, but every person can be part of the solution by learning about climate science, supporting clean energy, and making choices that reduce greenhouse gas emissions. Our future depends on how quickly and effectively we can work together to implement solutions while adapting to changes that are already happening.

Fortunately, people around the world have recognized this problem and are responding with incredible innovation and determination. We hope that what you learned about climate change will inspire and motivate you to play your part in saving our only planet.

Careers in Climate Change

If you care about protecting our planet and are curious about solving one of the world's biggest challenges, then careers dedicated to Climate Change might be perfect for you! There are many exciting jobs for people who want to help create a sustainable future. Here are just a few examples.

Climate Scientists studies how Earth's climate works, makes predictions about future climate changes, and analyzes data from weather stations, satellites, and ice cores.

Renewable Energy Engineers design and builds solar panels, wind turbines, and other clean energy systems that don't produce greenhouse gases.

Environmental Lawyers work on laws and policies to protect the environment and reduce greenhouse gas emissions.

Sustainability Consultants help businesses and organizations reduce their carbon footprint and operate in more environmentally friendly ways.

Urban Planners design cities and communities that can handle climate change impacts while reducing emissions through better transportation and green spaces.

Marine Biologists study how climate change affects ocean life, coral reefs, and sea creatures, and works on conservation projects.

Biologists work to protect plants and animals whose habitats are threatened by climate change, including reforestation and wildlife protection projects.

Architects design buildings that use less energy, produce their own renewable power, and are built with sustainable materials.

Home or Classroom Project Ideas

1. Create A Weather Journal

Keep a weather journal for a month and spot patterns over time. Each day, write the temperature, the weather (sunny, rainy, cloudy, etc.), and anything interesting you notice.

At the end of the month, discuss the patterns you noticed.

2. Model How Greenhouse Gasses Trap Heat

You will need:
- Two clear jars or cups
- Two thermometers
- Plastic wrap
- A sunny window

What to do:
- Place a thermometer in each jar.
- Cover one jar with plastic wrap.
- Put both jars in the sun for 30 minutes.
- Record the temperatures.

Discuss what happened?

3. Track Your Carbon Footprint

For seven days, mark the activity you did each day.

- Walked or biked instead of driving
- Turned off lights when leaving a room
- Read a book instead of watching TV
- Recycled something
- Ate a plant-based meal
- Composted food scraps

Can you improve your score next week?

Climate Change Glossary

A glossary is like a mini-dictionary of terms with definitions.

Here's a glossary of terms associated with Climate Change.

Adaptation - Changes that people, animals, and plants make to live better with climate change effects.

Atmosphere - The layer of gases that surrounds Earth and contains the air we breathe.

Biodiversity - The variety of different plants and animals living in an area.

Carbon Capture - Technology that removes carbon dioxide from the air and stores it safely underground.

Carbon Cycle - The natural process where carbon moves between the air, oceans, plants, and soil.

Carbon Dioxide - An invisible gas that traps heat in the atmosphere; the main greenhouse gas from human activities.

Carbon Footprint - The total amount of greenhouse gases that a person, family, or activity produces.

Climate - The pattern of weather that happens in a place over many years (30 years or more).

Climate Change - Long-term changes in Earth's temperature and weather patterns caused by human activities.

Climate Zones - Different areas of Earth with their own typical weather patterns (tropical, temperate, polar).

Conservation - Using natural resources carefully so they last longer and protecting the environment.

Coral Bleaching - When coral reefs turn white because ocean water stays too warm for too long.

Deforestation - Cutting down forests, which removes trees that absorb carbon dioxide from the air.

Drought - A long period of time with little or no rainfall.

Electric Vehicle - A car, truck, or bus that runs on electricity instead of gasoline or diesel fuel.

Emissions - Gases released into the air, especially greenhouse gases from burning fossil fuels.

Extreme Weather - Unusually severe weather events like very strong storms, heat waves, or floods.

Fossil Fuels - Coal, oil, and natural gas formed underground from ancient plants and animals.

Glaciers - Large masses of ice that form on mountains and move very slowly.

Global Warming - The increase in Earth's average temperature caused by extra greenhouse gases.

Greenhouse Effect - How certain gases in the atmosphere trap heat from the sun to keep Earth warm.

Greenhouse Gases - Invisible gases that trap heat in the atmosphere (carbon dioxide, methane, water vapor, nitrous oxide).

Hurricane - A large, powerful storm with very strong winds that forms over warm ocean water.

Hydroelectric - Electricity made using the power of flowing water.

Ice Caps - Large areas of ice that cover the North and South Poles.

Methane - A greenhouse gas produced by farm animals, rice fields, and decomposing waste.

Mitigation - Actions taken to reduce greenhouse gas emissions and slow climate change.

Nitrous Oxide - A greenhouse gas released from fertilizers and some industrial processes.

Ozone Layer - A protective layer of gas high in the atmosphere that blocks harmful sun rays.

Permafrost - Soil that stays frozen all year in very cold places like Alaska, Canada and Siberia.

Photosynthesis - The process plants use to make food from sunlight and carbon dioxide.

Polar Zones - The coldest areas of Earth near the North and South Poles.

Precipitation - Water that falls from the sky as rain, snow, sleet, or hail.

<u>Recycling</u> - Processing used materials to make new products instead of throwing them away.

<u>Reforestation</u> - Planting new trees to replace forests that were cut down.

<u>Renewable Energy</u> - Energy from sources that never run out, like sunlight, wind, and flowing water.

<u>Sea Level Rise</u> - The slow increase in ocean levels caused by melting ice and warming water.

<u>Solar Panels</u> - Devices that capture sunlight and turn it into electricity.

<u>Sustainability</u> - Meeting our needs today without harming the ability of future generations to meet their needs.

<u>Temperature</u> - How hot or cold something is, measured in degrees.

<u>Tornado</u> - A violent spinning column of air that can cause severe damage.

<u>Tropical Zone</u> - The warm area of Earth near the equator that stays hot all year.

<u>Weather</u> - What the atmosphere is like outside right now (sunny, rainy, hot, cold, etc.).

<u>Wind Turbines</u> - Large machines with spinning blades that use wind to generate electricity.

Climate Change Quiz

Multiple Choice

1. What is the main difference between weather and climate?
   a) Weather is hot, climate is cold
   b) Weather happens daily, climate is long-term patterns
   c) Weather is inside, climate is outside
   d) There is no difference

2. How long do scientists study weather patterns to understand climate?
   a) One year
   b) Five years
   c) Thirty years or more
   d) One hundred years

3. What percentage of global greenhouse gas emissions comes from electricity and heat generation?
   a) 15%
   b) 25%
   c) 35%
   d) 45%

4. Without greenhouse gases, Earth would be how much colder?
   a) 30 degrees Fahrenheit
   b) 45 degrees Fahrenheit
   c) 60 degrees Fahrenheit
   d) 75 degrees Fahrenheit

5. Which gas makes up about 76% of all greenhouse gas emissions?
   a) Methane
   b) Water vapor
   c) Carbon dioxide
   d) Nitrous oxide

6. How long does carbon dioxide stay in the atmosphere?
   a) A few months
   b) A few years
   c) Hundreds of years
   d) Forever

7. What causes coral bleaching in the Maldives?
   a) Ocean temperatures staying too warm for too long
   b) Too much sunlight
   c) Pollution from boats
   d) Overfishing

8. Which renewable energy source is now the cheapest in history?
   a) Wind power
   b) Solar power
   c) Hydroelectric power
   d) Nuclear power

9. How many miles can modern electric cars travel on a single charge?
   a) 100 miles
   b) 200 miles
   c) Over 300 miles
   d) 500 miles

10. What percentage of global emissions could be reduced if all cars were electric?
    a) 10%
    b) 16%
    c) 25%
    d) 30%

11. How much carbon dioxide does a single mature tree absorb per year?
    a) 24 pounds
    b) 36 pounds
    c) 48 pounds
    d) 60 pounds

12. How many trees did Ethiopia plant in a single day?
    a) 100 million
    b) 250 million
    c) Over 350 million
    d) 500 million

13. What happens when oceans absorb extra carbon dioxide?
    a) They become warmer
    b) They become more acidic
    c) They become saltier
    d) They become cleaner

14. Changes that used to take thousands of years are now happening in:
    a) Months
    b) Years
    c) Decades
    d) Centuries

15. Which zone stays warm all year?
    a) Polar zone
    b) Temperate zone
    c) Tropical zone
    d) Arctic zone

16. What do scientists study to learn about ancient climates?
    a) Old books
    b) Bubbles in ancient ice
    c) Rock formations
    d) Fossil fuels

17. How much faster are Himalayan glaciers melting now compared to the early 2000s?
    a) Same speed
    b) Twice as fast
    c) Three times as fast
    d) Four times as fast

18. What percentage of emissions comes from transportation?
    a) 14%
    b) 18%
    c) 24%
    d) 30%

19. What is the greenhouse effect most similar to?
    a) A fan cooling you down
    b) A blanket keeping you warm
    c) An umbrella blocking rain
    d) A window letting in light

20. Which sector contributes 24% of global emissions?
    a) Transportation only
    b) Buildings only
    c) Agriculture and Land Use
    d) Industry only

<u>Fill in the Blank</u>

21. Lila and Andy have been keeping a _____ journal for three years.

22. The Maldives are a chain of tropical islands in the _____ Ocean.

23. Climate is the pattern of weather that occurs over a _____ time.

24. The _____ zone near the equator stays warm all year.

25. Scientists collect weather information for _____ years or more to study climate.

26. Earth uses invisible _____ in the atmosphere to stay warm.

27. The main greenhouse gases include water vapor, carbon dioxide, methane, and _____ oxide.

28. Fossil fuels formed underground over millions of _____.

29. When farmers raise cattle and sheep, these animals produce _____ gas.

30. Carbon dioxide stays in the atmosphere for hundreds of _____.

31. There is now more carbon dioxide in the air than there has been for over _____ million years.

32. Some coastal areas that were once dry now _____ during storms.

33. Spring is arriving _____ in many parts of the world.

34. _____ panels capture energy from sunlight without producing greenhouse gases.

35. Wind _____ use moving air to generate power.

36. Electric vehicles produce no _____ while driving.

37. Scientists are developing methods to _____ carbon dioxide directly from the air.

38. Farmers plant _____ crops that absorb carbon dioxide.

39. Cities are adding bike lanes and _____ transportation to reduce emissions.

40. Simple actions like walking or _____ instead of driving help reduce greenhouse gases.

41. Weather and climate mean exactly the same thing.

42. The polar zones near the North and South Poles stay mostly cold.

43. Earth's climate has been remarkably stable for thousands of years.

44. The greenhouse effect is harmful to life on Earth.

45. Venus is too hot and Mars is too cold compared to Earth.

46. Burning fossil fuels releases carbon dioxide into the atmosphere.

47. Deforestation increases the number of trees that absorb carbon dioxide.

48. The last decade included some of the warmest years ever recorded.

49. Mountain glaciers are growing larger due to climate change.

50. Ocean water is getting warmer and more acidic.

51. Birds are migrating at the same times they always have.

52. Renewable energy sources are becoming more expensive over time.

53. Electric cars can travel hundreds of miles on a single charge.

54. Buildings are becoming less energy efficient.

55. Every person can be part of the climate solution.

Quiz Answers

Multiple Choice	Fill in the Blank	True/False
1. b	21. weather	41. False
2. c	22. Indian	42. True
3. b	23. long	43. True
4. c	24. tropical	44. False
5. c	25. thirty	45. True
6. c	26. gases	46. True
7. a	27. nitrous	47. False
8. b	28. years	48. True
9. c	29. methane	49. False
10. b	30. years	50. True
11. c	31. 3	51. False
12. c	32. flood	52. False
13. b	33. earlier	53. True
14. c	34. Solar	54. False
15. c	35. turbines	55. True
16. b	36. emissions	
17. b	37. capture	
18. c	38. cover	
19. b	39. public	
20. c	40. biking	

Take a look at other subjects Lila and Andy are learning about...

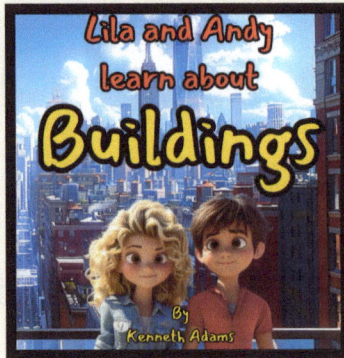
Lila and Andy learn about **Buildings**
By Kenneth Adams

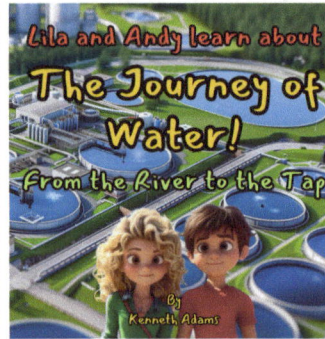
Lila and Andy learn about **The Journey of Water!**
From the River to the Tap

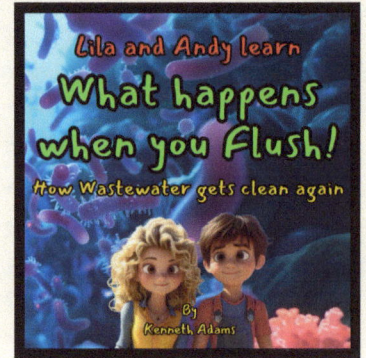
Lila and Andy learn **What happens when you Flush!**
How Wastewater gets clean again

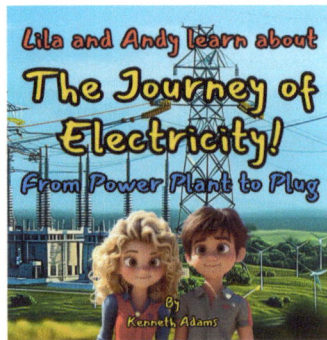
Lila and Andy learn about **The Journey of Electricity!**
From Power Plant to Plug
By Kenneth Adams

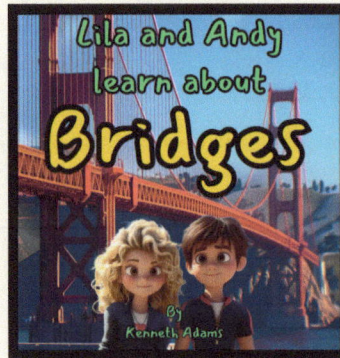
Lila and Andy learn about **Bridges**
By Kenneth Adams

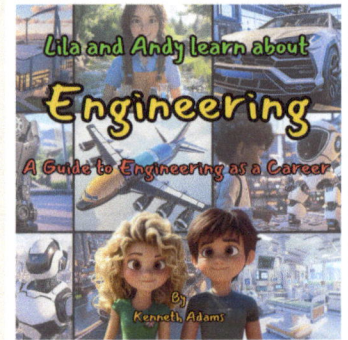
Lila and Andy learn about **Engineering**
A Guide to Engineering as a Career
By Kenneth Adams

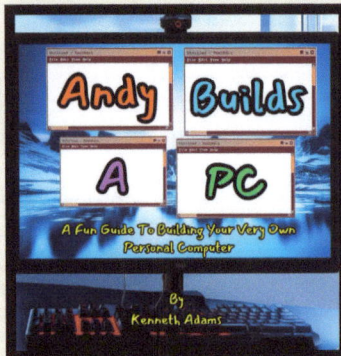
Andy Builds A PC
A Fun Guide To Building Your Very Own Personal Computer
By Kenneth Adams

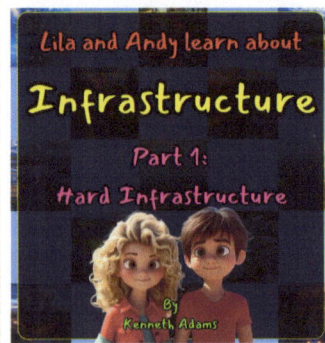
Lila and Andy learn about **Infrastructure**
Part 1: Hard Infrastructure
By Kenneth Adams

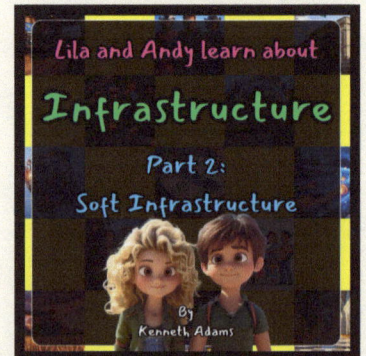
Lila and Andy learn about **Infrastructure**
Part 2: Soft Infrastructure
By Kenneth Adams

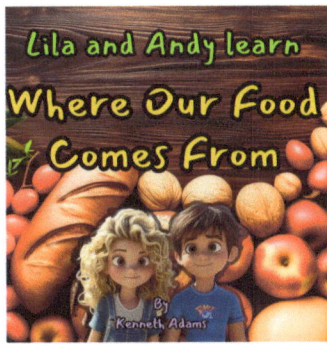
Lila and Andy learn
Where Our Food
Comes From
By
Kenneth Adams

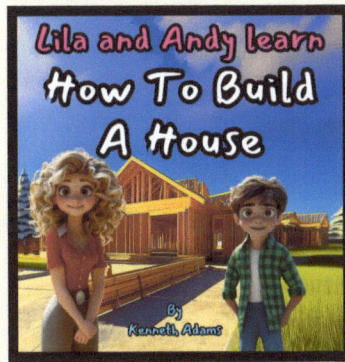
Lila and Andy learn
How To Build
A House
By
Kenneth Adams

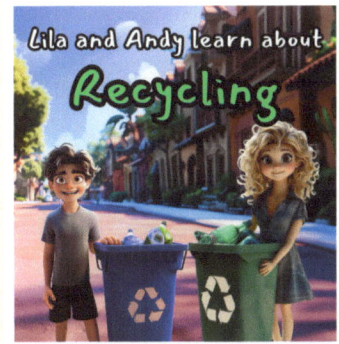
Lila and Andy learn about
Recycling

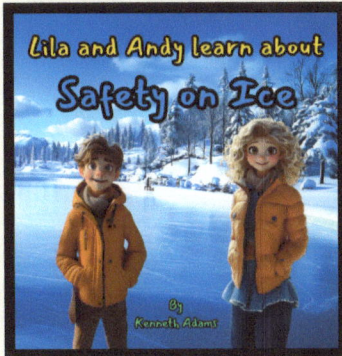
Lila and Andy learn about
Safety on Ice
By
Kenneth Adams

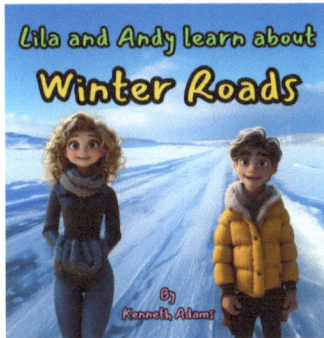
Lila and Andy learn about
Winter Roads
By
Kenneth Adams

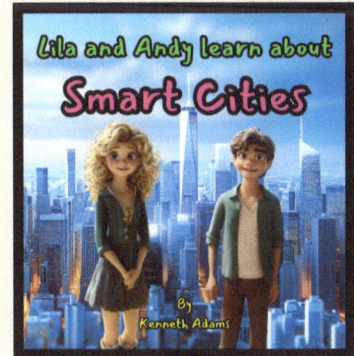
Lila and Andy learn about
Smart Cities
By
Kenneth Adams

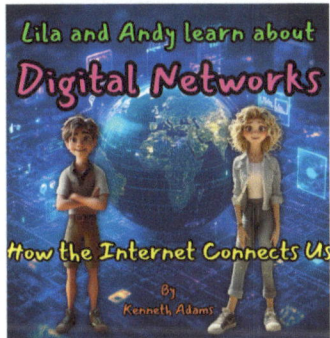
Lila and Andy learn about
Digital Networks
How the Internet Connects Us
By
Kenneth Adams

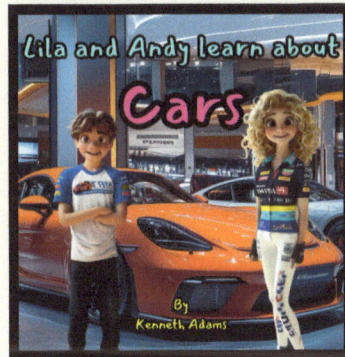
Lila and Andy learn about
Cars
By
Kenneth Adams

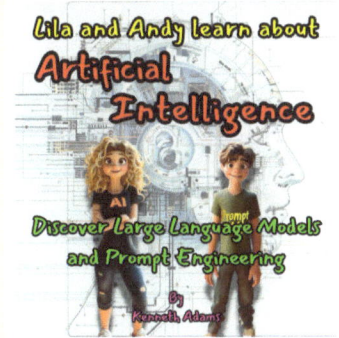
Lila and Andy learn about
Artificial
Intelligence
Discover Large Language Models
and Prompt Engineering
By
Kenneth Adams

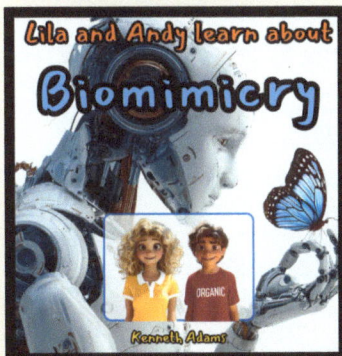
Lila and Andy learn about
Biomimicry
Kenneth Adams

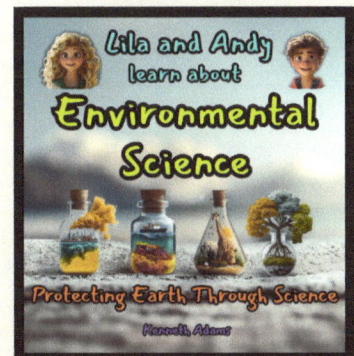
Lila and Andy
learn about
Environmental
Science
Protecting Earth Through Science
Kenneth Adams

www.ingramcontent.com/pod-product-compliance
Lightning Source LLC
Chambersburg PA
CBHW042013080426
42734CB00003B/69

9 781998 552245